Contents

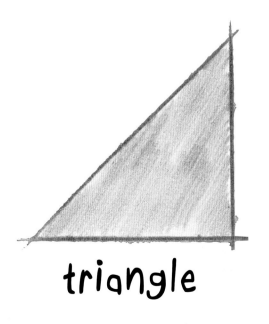

triangle

wooden blocks

How many eyes does Betty bear have?

How to use this book

round clock

Number skills are very important in today's world. This book will give children a head start in learning essential pre-school skills such as counting, matching and recognising patterns. It offers plenty of practice at counting from one to ten, before moving on to concepts such as odd and even numbers. Bright, colourful photographs of familiar objects help bring the pages to life, so that counting and adding become concrete activities concerned with real objects.

square clock

Can you see the number 30?

padlock

sign

4

What numbers can you see on the tape measure?

Jim Bear

Young children love looking at pictures and naming what they see. It is even more fun for them to share a book with an adult. You could count with them, and help them match up the pairs or spot the odd one out. Use the questions round the edges of each page to start a conversation and encourage the child to study the pictures more closely.

Children will love searching for the teddy bear on each page.

Betty Bear

tape measure

How many ears does the rabbit have?

Count the rabbit!

What number comes after one?

What colour is the rabbit?

one

6

How many paws does the rabbit have?

two ears

one nose

one white rabbit

four grey paws

What colour are the rabbit's paws?

Count the kittens!

two

How many eyes have the kittens altogether?

two ears

one grey kitten

two
kittens

two ears

one white kitten

How many car doors can you see?

Count the toy cars!

three

3

How many green cars are there?

What number comes before three?

Are there more green cars or blue cars?

three toy cars

green car

blue car

green car

How many wheels can you see?

What number comes after three?

How many noses have the puppies altogether?

Count the puppies!

How many puppies are brown?

What number comes before four?

four

Are there more brown puppies or white puppies?

black and white puppy

brown puppy

four puppies

brown puppy

white puppy

What colour are the puppies' noses?

What number comes after four?

13

Count the fish!

five

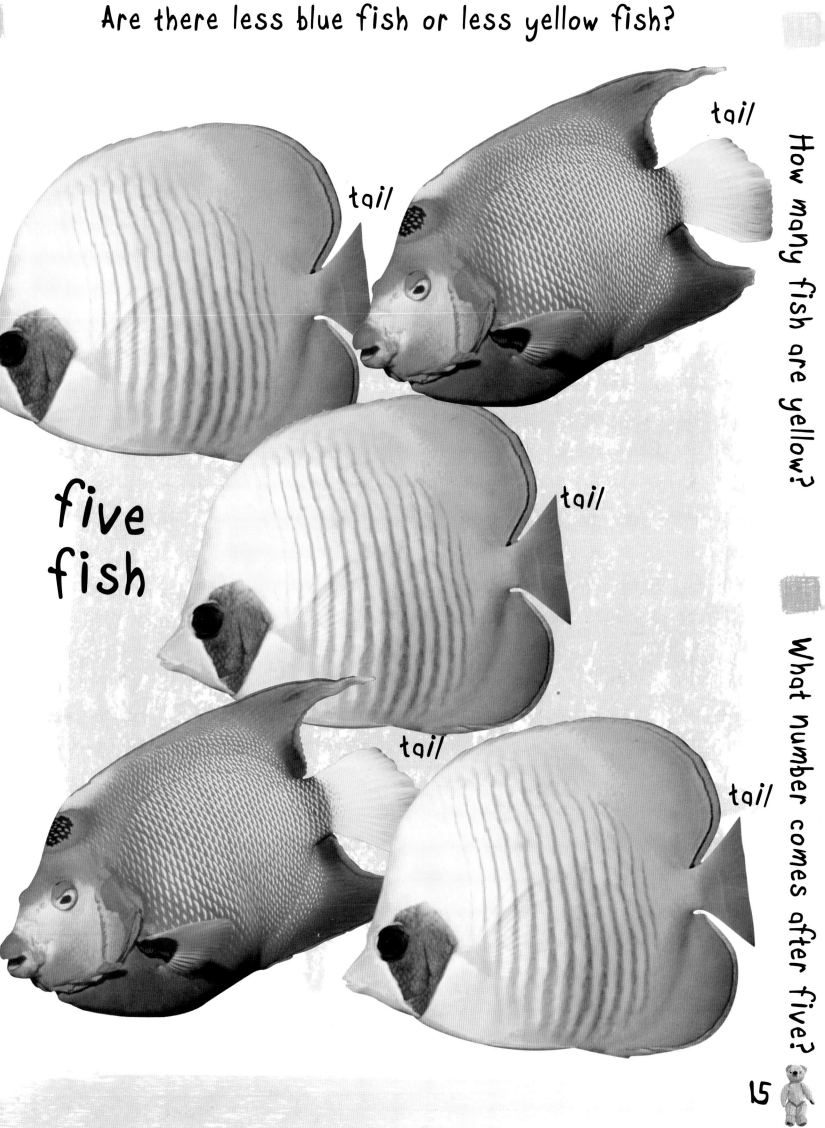

Are there less blue fish or less yellow fish?

tail

tail

five
fish

tail

tail

tail

How many fish are yellow?

What number comes after five?

Count the birds!

six

What number comes before six?

How many green birds can you find?

beak

one flying bird

beak

beak

six birds

one flying bird

beak

beak

beak

How many bird beaks can you see? What number comes after six?

17

Are there more brown horses or more spotted horses?

Count the horses!

How many horses are black?

What number comes before seven?

seven

How many hooves does a horse have?

seven horses

one spotted horse

hooves

hooves

one spotted horse

Count the soft toys!

How many toy lions can you see?

What number comes before eight?

eight

20

Are there more bears or less bears than lions?

eight soft toys

Count the toy animals!

nine

How many animals are just one colour?

giraffe

elephant

Which animal has tusks?

panda

gorilla

deer

zebra

lion

What number comes after nine?

bear

lioness

nine toy animals

23

How many butterflies have yellow wings?

Count the butterflies!

ten

How many butterflies have green wings?

How many butterflies have green wings? What number comes before ten?

ten butterflies

How many butterflies are not yellow?

What number comes after ten?

Number line!

What number comes before two?

What number comes after three?

1 2 3 4 5

one   two   three   four   five

one
pencil

two
puppies

three
kittens

four
globes

five
frogs

Count from one to ten

6 7 8 9 10

six seven eight nine ten

six
cherries

seven
torches

eight
ducks

nine
sunflowers

ten
basketballs

Are there more lemons or more pineapples?

One to ten

Can you count out each group of fruit from one to ten?

How many green fruits are there?

How many orange fruits are there?

1 orange

2 apples

3 bananas

4 lemons

5 limes

6 tomatoes

28

Are there less bananas or less kiwi fruits?

How far can you count on after ten?

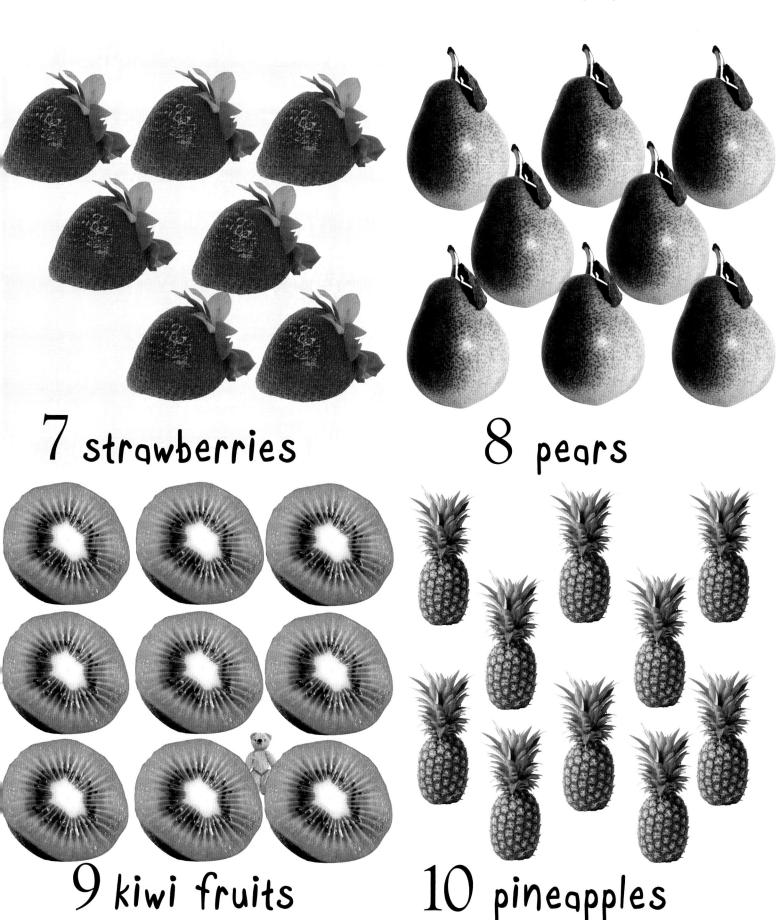

7 strawberries

8 pears

9 kiwi fruits

10 pineapples

How many round fruits are there?

Count the animals

Count out how many of each animal you can see.

How many penguins are there?

How many parrots are there?

penguins

tigers

polar bears

antelopes

30

If there were one more panda, how many would there be?

How many black and white animals can you see?

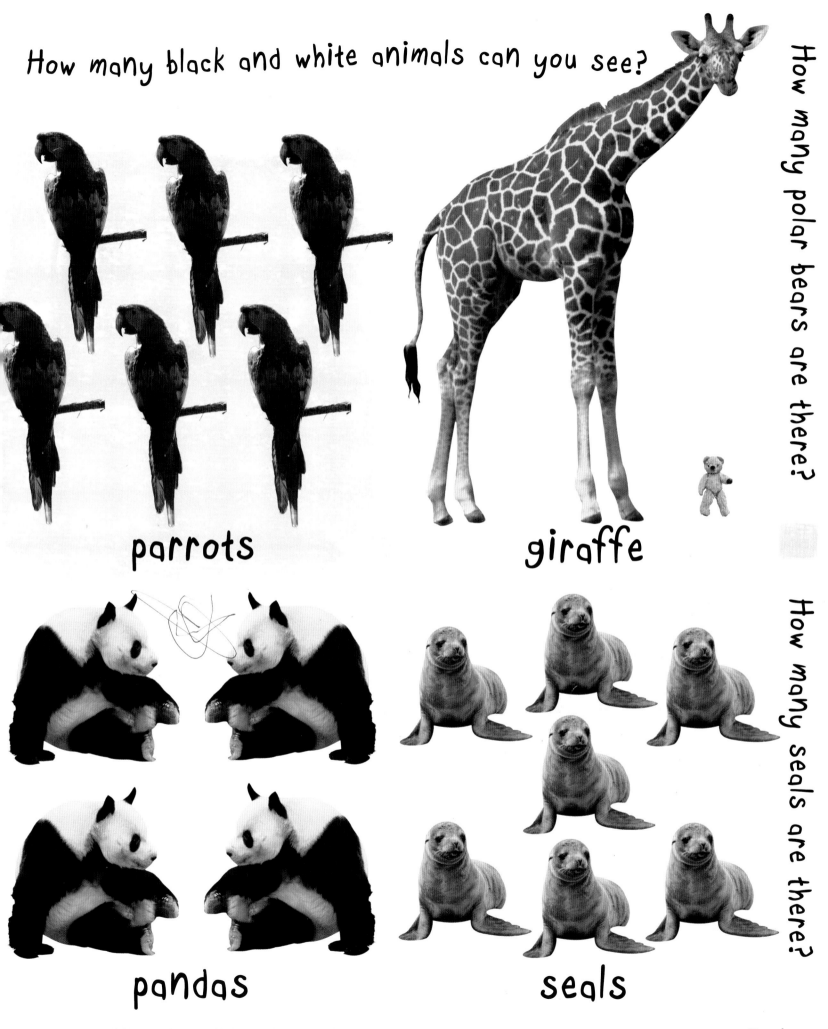

parrots

giraffe

pandas

seals

What number is missing from the telephone?

Missing numbers

Can you see which numbers are missing?

How many number 5s can you see?

How many teddy bears are there?

telephone

tape measure

1 2 3 4 5 7 8 9 10 11 12

What number is missing from the TV remote?

What number is missing from the number blocks?

TV remote

number blocks

clock

dice

What number is missing from the clock?   How many dots are on the dice?

33

Even numbers

Even numbers always come in pairs.

Is there an even number before two?

How many tractors are there?

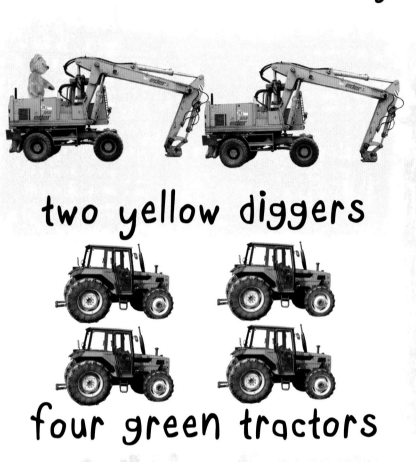

two yellow diggers

four green tractors

six blue tractors

eight orange diggers

ten red road rollers

34

Odd numbers

Odd numbers always have an odd one out.

one toy aeroplane

three toy trains

five toy boats

seven toy cars

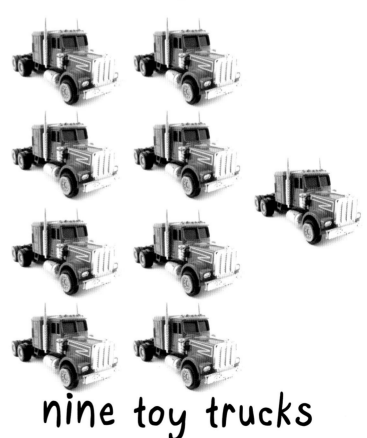

nine toy trucks

Do odd numbers come in pairs?   What is the next odd number after nine?

35

Shapes

How many sides does each shape have?

Which shape has three sides?

Which shape have five sides?

Does a hexagon have five sides?

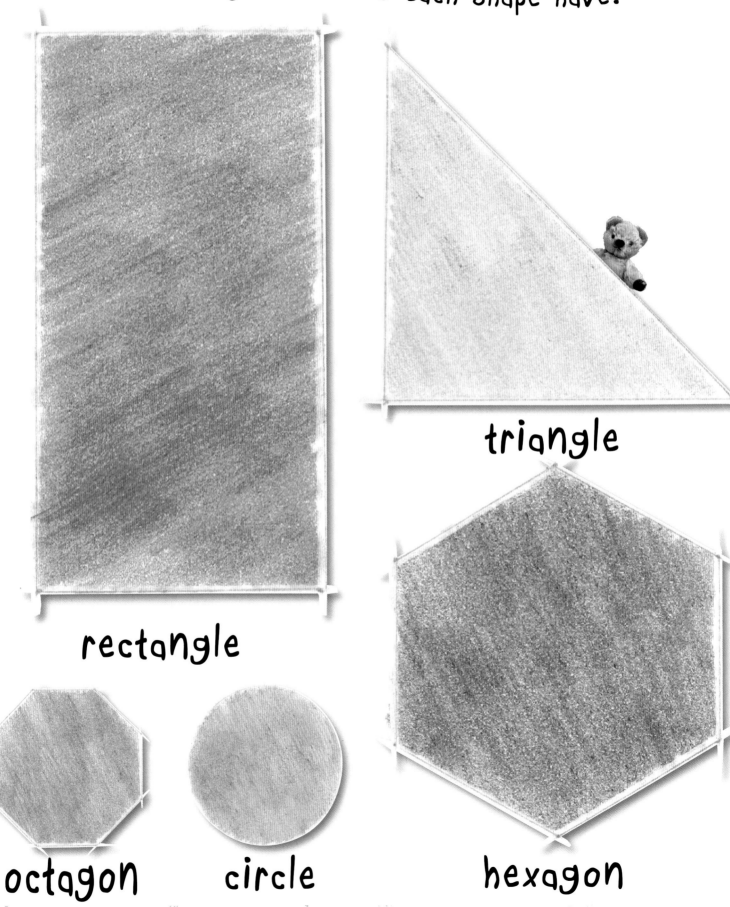

rectangle

triangle

octagon

circle

hexagon

Do some shapes have the same number of sides?

Which shape has the most sides?

pentagon

square

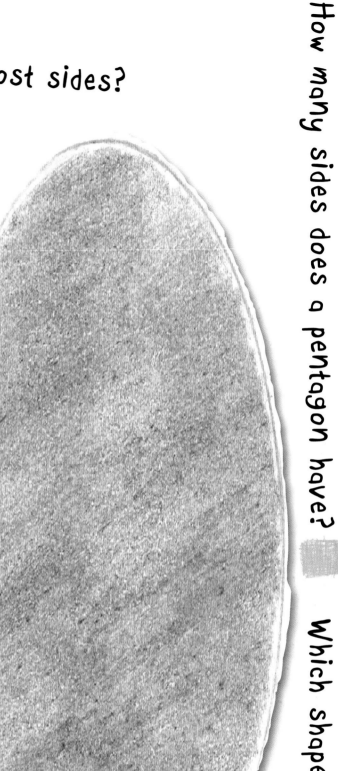

oval

Which triangle is the largest?

Which square is the smallest?

six triangles

How many squares are there?

five squares

38

Is there an odd or an even number of circles?

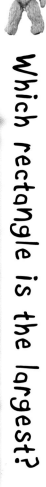

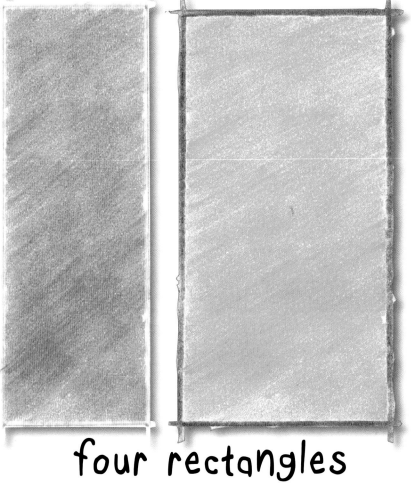

four rectangles

eight circles

Which rectangle is the largest?

How many circles are there?

Pattern problems

Can you see the patterns?

How many bars of soap are there?

What colour will the next bar of soap be?

1 3 5 ?

What number will come next?

How many balloons are there?

What colour will the next toy boat be?

What shape will come next?

40

How many footballs are there?

Can you see the patterns?

What toy will come next?

What shape will come next?

What colour ball will come next?

2 4 6 8 ?

What number will come next?

How many squares are there?

Is there an even number of puppets?

What is the opposite of sad?

Opposites

Opposites are things that are very different from each other.

Can you see a fast car?

sad boy   happy boy

short pencil

long pencil

Do happy boys smile or cry?

fast car

slow car

open book

closed book

What is the opposite of big?

Can you think of any more opposites?

car front

small tree

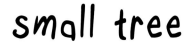

car back

big tree

clean boots

dirty boots

empty glass

full glass

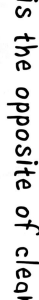

What is the opposite of clean?

43

Can you find a pair of lawn mowers?

Match the pairs

Two things that are the same make a pair.

Is there a pair of step ladders?

 step ladder

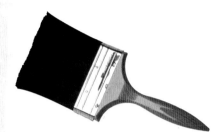 paintbrush

 bucket

 toolbox

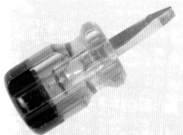 screwdriver

 tape measure

 lawn mower

Can you see a pair of buckets?

 lawn mower

 tape measure

 step ladder

 toolbox

 bucket

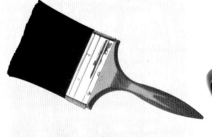 paintbrush

 screwdriver

44

Musical instruments

How many pairs of musical instruments can you see?

Match the pairs of instruments.

Can you find a pair of trombones?

Can you find a pair of violins?

keyboard

banjo

violin

tambourine

guitar

tambourine

banjo

drum

trombone

keyboard

violin

drum

guitar

trombone

Are there less ducklings or less zebras?

Number jumble

Can you match each number to an animal picture?

Is there an odd number of ducklings?

How many cheetahs are there?

1 2 3 4 5

cheetahs

cockerel

ducklings

hens

46

Are there more hippos or more elephants?

Can you match each number to an animal picture?

6 7 8 9 10

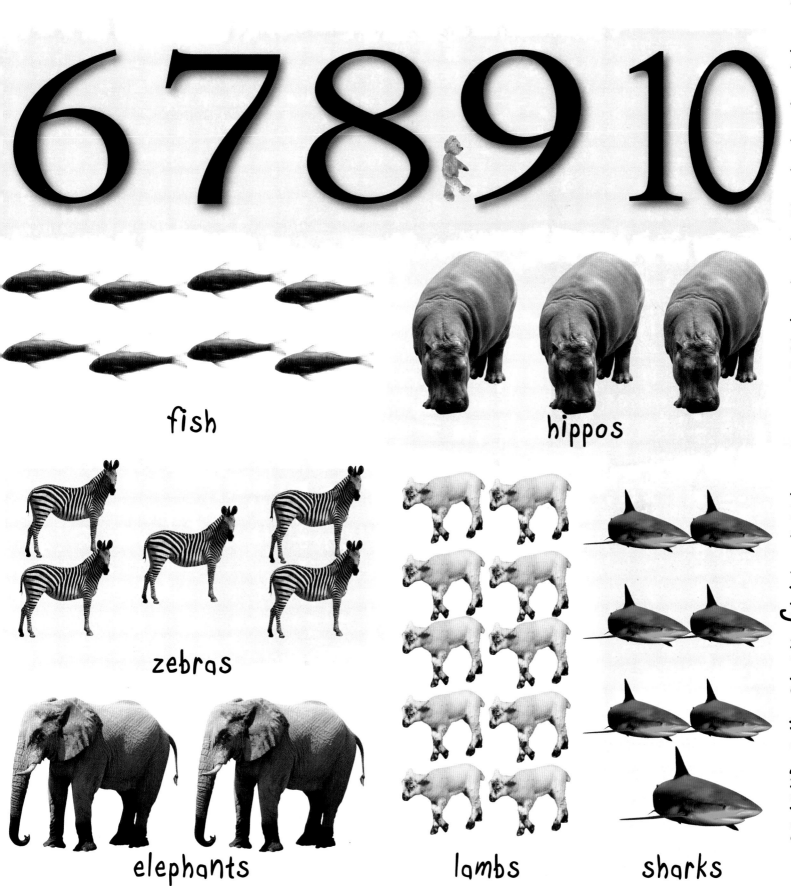

fish

hippos

zebras

lambs

elephants

lambs

sharks

Are there odd numbers and even numbers on the clock?

A clock!

Can you count around the clock
starting at one?

What number comes after two?

www.scribblersbooks.com

Created and designed by:
Rob Walker

Consultant: Monica Hughes
is an Educational Advisor and
author of many books for young
children. She has been
Headteacher of a First School,
Primary Advisory Teacher and
Senior Lecturer in Early
Childhood Education.

Published in Great Britain 2009 by
Scribblers, a division of Book House,
25 Marlborough Place,
Brighton
BN1 1UB

Telephone: 01273 603306
Facsimile: 01273 621619

A CIP catalogue record for this book is
available from the British Library.

Printed and bound in China.